# OWLS

*by Josh Gregory*

**Children's Press®**

An Imprint of Scholastic Inc.
New York   Toronto   London   Auckland   Sydney
Mexico City   New Delhi   Hong Kong
Danbury, Connecticut

Content Consultant
Dr. Stephen S. Ditchkoff
Professor of Wildlife Sciences
Auburn University
Auburn, Alabama

Photographs © 2013: age fotostock/DESMETTE FREDE: 11; Alamy
Images: 36 (David Tipling), 40 (Doug McCutcheon), 27 (James
Osmond); Bob Italiano: 44 foreground, 45 foreground; Dreamstime: 1,
46 (Alvinge), 2 background, 3, 44 background, 45 background (Lakis
Fourouklas); iStockphoto: 4, 5 background, 20 (Abdolhamid Ebrahimi),
5 top, 8 (David Garry); Media Bakery: 15 (Jeremy Woodhouse), 12
(Paul E. Tessier), 35 (Warren Jacobi); Shutterstock, Inc./mountainpix: 32;
Superstock, Inc.: 24, 31 (age fotostock), 23 (JTB Photo Communications),
19, 28 (Minden Pictures), 5 bottom, 16 (Wayne Lynch/All Canada
Photos); The Image Works/Nill/ullstein bild: 2 foreground, 7; Visuals
Unlimited/Bence Mate: cover; Yay Images/pictureguy: 39.

Library of Congress Cataloging-in-Publication Data
Gregory, Josh.
  Owls / by Josh Gregory.
     pages  cm.—(Nature's children)
  Includes bibliographical references and index.
  Audience: Ages 9–12.
  Audience: Grades 4–6.
  ISBN 978-0-531-20979-0 (lib. bdg.)
  ISBN 978-0-531-24305-3 (pbk.)
1. Owls—Juvenile literature. I. Title.
  QL696.S8G74 2013
  598.9'7—dc23          2012034329

All rights reserved. Published in 2013 by Children's Press, an imprint
of Scholastic Inc.
Printed in the United States of America 141
SCHOLASTIC, CHILDREN'S PRESS, and associated logos are
trademarks and/or registered trademarks of Scholastic Inc.

1 2 3 4 5 6 7 8 9 10 R 22 21 20 19 18 17 16 15 14 13

# Owls

| | |
|---|---|
| **Class** | Aves |
| **Order** | Strigiformes |
| **Family** | Strigidae (typical owls), Tytonidae (barn owls) |
| **Genus** | 25 *Strigidae* genera, 2 *Tytonidae* genera |
| **Species** | More than 200 species |
| **World distribution** | Found throughout all continents except Antarctica |
| **Habitat** | Owls can be found in almost every kind of land habitat, from deserts to rain forests to the Arctic |
| **Distinctive physical characteristics** | Flat faces; large eyes that face forward; small, hooked beaks; some species have tufts of feathers around their ears |
| **Habits** | Most are nocturnal; some are active around dawn and dusk; few species are active during the day; some species mate for life, while others find new mates each year; when food is especially plentiful, some species occasionally mate with multiple partners in a single breeding season |
| **Diet** | All species are carnivorous; smaller species mainly eat insects; large owls have been known to attack young deer; some species mainly eat fish |

# Contents

# CHAPTER 1

# Night Flight

On a dark, quiet night, a small mouse scurries across the forest floor. Up above, an owl turns its head to track the mouse's movement. Suddenly, the bird swoops down toward its target. Before the mouse even has time to react, the owl snatches it in its powerful **talons** and returns to the treetops. It has been another successful hunt.

There are more than 200 different **species** of owls on Earth. These incredible hunters range widely in size. The smallest is the elf owl, which grows to weigh only about 1.5 ounces (42.5 grams). Elf owls are around 6 inches (15 centimeters) long and have a wingspan of about 15 inches (38 cm). The largest species is the Eurasian eagle owl. It can reach lengths of about 28 inches (71 cm) and has a wingspan of around 5 feet (1.5 meters). This massive owl can weigh up to about 10 pounds (4.5 kilograms). That is more than 100 times heavier than an elf owl!

Adult Male
6 ft. (1.8 m)

Elf owl
15 inches (38 cm)

Eurasian eagle owl
5 feet (1.5 m)

*Boreal owls hunt mice and other small animals.*

# A Unique Appearance

Owls have a distinctive face shape that sets them apart from other types of birds. Most birds have long faces with one eye on each side of their head. Owls, however, have flat faces, and both of their eyes face forward. These eyes are very large in relation to the size of the owl's head. An owl's beak, on the other hand, is usually quite small compared to the size of its face. This sharp beak curves down and inward. Its powerful bite allows the owl to kill **prey** that survives the grasp of its sharp talons.

While all owls share these general characteristics, each species looks slightly different from the others. Some have eyes that are almost entirely black, while others have dark **pupils** ringed by shades of yellow and orange. Some species have short tufts of feathers on either side of the head, making it look as though they have horns.

FUN FACT!

An owl can hear a mouse walking from 75 feet (23 m) away.

*Some owls, such as the eagle owl, have bright orange eyes.*

# Colorful Coverings

Like other kinds of birds, owls are covered in feathers. These incredible body coverings allow owls to fly and help protect them from the weather. Owls have very short tail feathers compared to many other birds. Their wing feathers have a rounded shape.

Owl feathers lack the bright, vivid colors of many other types of birds. Instead, they come in various shades of white, brown, and gray. These colors combine to form a wide range of patterns. Some owls are mostly dark with lighter spots covering their bodies. Others have one pattern on their wings and another on their breasts. Some are almost entirely covered in a single solid color. These colors and patterns set different species of owls apart from one another. But just because two owls are part of the same species doesn't mean they have the same coloring. Owls in one region often display patterns different from those of their relatives living in faraway **habitats**.

*Barn owls are generally light colored, with white and light brown or orange feathers.*

# All Around the World

No matter where in the world you live, there are probably owls somewhere near your home. Owls are found on every continent except Antarctica. This means that different owl species live in a wide range of environments. Owls live everywhere from dry, dusty deserts to lush, green tropical rain forests. They live on mountains, in swamps, and on islands.

Each kind of owl is equipped with a variety of behaviors and physical features to help it survive in its habitat. Snowy owls, which live in freezing cold climates, have thicker feathers than most other owl species. This helps keep them warm in the harsh, icy weather. When owls get too hot, they can vibrate the muscles in their necks to help circulate air through their mouths. This is similar to the way dogs pant when they are hot.

**FUN FACT!** Even a snowy owl's bill and toes are covered with feathers.

*A snowy owl's thick covering of feathers helps it stay warm in its icy habitat.*

# CHAPTER 2

# Hunters in the Darkness

Most owls are **nocturnal**. They sleep during the day and hunt at night, when the darkness can help them stay hidden. Some species, however, hunt during the day. Others are most active just before sunrise and just after sunset. No matter what time of day they prefer to hunt, owls are effective **predators**.

Depending on where they live, different kinds of owls use different methods of hunting. Owls that live in areas with lots of trees spend their time waiting in the branches for prey to pass beneath them. Those that live near water hunt by flying above and looking out for fish that swim close to the surface. Some owl species prefer to hunt in large, open areas. They fly around in circles, searching the ground below for unsuspecting prey. When an owl has located a tasty treat, it dives down and snatches the target in its talons. Then it carries its meal off to a quiet location where it can eat without being disturbed.

*The Blakiston's fish owl of Japan is named for its favorite food—fish.*

# What's on the Menu?

Owls are carnivores. All of their food comes from the prey they hunt. Smaller species, such as the elf owl and the whiskered owl, live on diets that consist mainly of insects. Large owls must hunt much bigger prey to get enough food. Some species are even strong enough to snatch small deer. Most owl species prefer to eat rodents such as mice, rats, or squirrels.

Usually, owls open their beaks wide and swallow their prey whole. Their bodies digest as much of the meal as possible. However, owls cannot digest bones, hair, teeth, and certain other body parts. Their bodies compress these leftover parts into hard lumps called owl pellets. The owl regurgitates these pellets after it has finished digesting its meal.

When an owl catches prey that is too big to swallow whole, it uses its sharp beak to tear off pieces of meat. Owls often leave behind clean skeletons after picking off every bit they can swallow.

*Pygmy owls usually hunt insects and other small animals during the evening.*

# Sound and Vision

Owls have incredible senses that help them hunt down prey at night. Their eyes are large enough to absorb even the smallest amount of light. This is what allows them to see in the dark. An owl's eyes are so large that they cannot move around in the bird's eye sockets. Owls must turn their heads in order to look around. To make up for this limitation, they can turn their heads about three-quarters of the way around.

An owl's sense of hearing is just as important as its vision. Though it may look like the sides of their heads are smooth, owls actually have huge ears beneath their feathers. The shape of the owl's face helps direct sound into these ear holes. The two ear holes have slightly different shapes, and one is located higher on the owl's head. This unique ear structure allows them to locate exactly where a sound is coming from. Certain species can locate prey entirely by sound.

*Owls can look behind themselves without turning their bodies.*

# Owls in Motion

Owls generally travel by flying. Most do not fly long distances or rise very high in the sky. They simply move from tree to tree or from a tree to the ground. Owls that live in large, open areas tend to spend more time in the air than forest-dwelling species. These species usually have larger wings than those that spend less time in flight. Larger wings require less flapping to keep the bird in the air. This allows the owl to save energy as it searches for prey.

Some owls do not need to fly very often. Burrowing owls live in holes in the ground and spend very little time in trees. As a result, they are very good at traveling along the ground on foot. Most other types of owls use their feet mainly for capturing prey and perching.

*Short-eared owls can often be seen flying above open spaces, even during the daytime.*

# Incredible Feathers

Even though they hunt in the dark, owls have a little extra help to avoid being seen. The colored patterns of their feathers often act as camouflage to help them blend in with their environments. For example, owls that live in snowy areas are usually white. Those that live in forests have striped or spotted patterns to help them blend in with leaves and bark.

An owl's feathers help it stay silent when it swoops down on its prey. The edges of the wing feathers have a special shape that muffles the sound of air moving over the wings. This means that prey animals often don't know they are targets until it is too late to get away.

Owls also use their feathers to keep warm. Species living in cold regions often have extra feathers on their legs. Scientists believe this is to help them avoid losing too much heat.

*Camouflage helps this Ural owl blend in with its forest home.*

# CHAPTER 3

# An Owl's Life

Most owl species do not usually spend much time in the company of other owls. They live mainly solitary lives, and some species are territorial. The only time they come together is when they need to find mates. Males often gain the trust of females by dropping gifts of food near them. They also work to drive away other males. In addition, some species make noises or display their wings in special flight patterns to attract females.

Many owl species form long-term pair bonds. This means that the same male and female mate every year. They usually share the same territory year-round and meet up at the start of each annual mating season.

Pair bonds are often monogamous. Some, however, mate with other owls in addition to their main partners.

*Eastern screech owls, like these two, usually form monogamous pair bonds that sometimes last their entire lives.*

# From Eggs to Chicks

Owls do not usually build their own nests. Instead, they look for hidden places where they can lay their eggs safely. Some owls find holes in trees. Others make use of the previously used nests of other birds. Certain owl species lay their eggs on the ground. A mother owl lays anywhere from 1 to 14 eggs during a breeding season. She does not lay them all at once, though. On average, most female owls lay one egg every two days. This means it can take several weeks for a mother to finish laying her eggs.

The mother and father owls take turns sitting on the eggs to keep them warm. While one parent stays in the nest, the other often goes off to hunt and bring back food to share. It takes anywhere from two to five weeks for eggs to begin hatching, depending on the species. The eggs that were laid first are the first to hatch.

*A nest of eggs always has a parent owl nearby.*

# Learning and Growing

Owl parents hunt and bring back food for their new babies. The oldest owl chicks in a clutch have the best chance of surviving. If there are not enough prey animals in the area, the younger chicks usually starve. Their stronger, older brothers and sisters overpower them and eat all of the food.

Most owl chicks look very different from their parents at first. They have different coloring and soft, fuzzy feathers. As the chicks get older and larger, new types of feathers begin to grow in. After about two months, they are able to leave the nest. They start learning how to fly and hunt for food, but they do not move too far away from their parents. After about another month, they are ready to leave the nest for good. The young owls fly off to find their own territory and eventually have chicks of their own.

*The more chicks there are in a clutch, the more competition there is for something to eat.*

# Speaking Up

Owls make a variety of noises to communicate with one another. Each species produces a different range of vocal sounds. These can include quiet purrs, songlike chirps and whistles, or ear-piercing screeches. Owls are most known, however, for their unique hooting sounds. Larger species produce lower, deeper sounds than smaller ones do. Males produce lower sounds than females do. Owls can also make noise by clicking their beaks or clapping their wings together. Some sounds are meant to warn away other owls, while other sounds are for attracting mates. Chicks make noises to get their parents' attention.

An owl's body language serves as another important form of communication. Pair-bonded owls often touch and preen each other as a sign of affection. Male and female owls sometimes rub their bills and faces together during courtship. Owls also use body language to fend off potential threats. Some species extend their wings and puff themselves up to look bigger in order to scare away other owls.

*A great horned owl's call can be heard for miles around.*

# CHAPTER 4

# The Family Tree

Owls have lived on Earth for at least 65.5 million years. The oldest owl fossils that scientists have discovered date back to this time. These fossils come from an extinct owl species known as *Ogygoptynx*. So far, scientists have only found fossils of this mysterious bird's ankle and foot. Some experts believe that even older owl species may have existed, but they have not yet discovered any fossils to prove it.

Most ancient owl species are now extinct. Many of them were very different from today's owls. The largest known owl species was *Ornimegalonyx*. This massive owl grew to be more than 3 feet (0.9 m) tall. It lived from about two million to three million years ago in what is now Cuba in the Caribbean Sea. Scientists believe that this giant owl could take down prey weighing as much as 110 pounds (50 kg).

*Owls played a large role in ancient Egyptian culture.*

# Two Types

Scientists organize all of today's owl species into two different families. The vast majority of owl species belong to the *Strigidae* family. They are known as typical owls. Around 16 other owl species belong to the *Tytonidae* family. They are called barn owls. Barn owls look slightly different from typical owls. Their faces are shaped like hearts, and none of them have ear tufts. They also have smaller eyes than typical owls do. All of them have light-colored feathers. Because of their unique appearance, some people call them monkey-faced owls.

Barn owls get their name from their habit of nesting in barns and other man-made structures. Farmers like to have them around because they eat mice, rats, and other pests that can ruin crops. However, not all barn owls live on farms. They also nest in the same places that other owls do, including hollow trees and abandoned bird nests.

*Barn owls are known for making their homes in or around farm buildings.*

# Close Relatives

Scientists once believed that owls were most closely related to other large birds of prey, such as hawks and eagles. However, most experts now think that an owl's nearest relative is the nightjar. There are somewhere between 60 and 70 species of these small birds. Like owls, they are carnivorous hunters. However, they are not big enough to hunt for rodents or other large prey. Instead, they survive on a diet of insects.

Nightjars are excellent flyers and can pull off a variety of quick twists and turns as they jet through the sky in search of moths, flies, and other tasty snacks. They can also fly silently, just as owls do. A nightjar's favorite times to hunt are right before sunrise and just as the sun is setting. Unlike other birds, the middle claw on a nightjar's foot is serrated. It uses this unique feature like a comb when it preens.

*Nightjars are colored in shades of gray, brown, and reddish brown.*

# CHAPTER 5

# Living with Owls

For hundreds of years, humans have seen owls as symbols of mystery and darkness. Many ancient cultures feared them. But owls are no danger to humans. In fact, many people never even get a chance to see owls in the wild because most are only active at night.

Even though we might not see them regularly, many owls live in the same places people live. They are common near farms, small towns, and even in big cities. Owls can be very beneficial to humans. The prey they like most, such as insects and rodents, are typically pest animals that people do not like. Owls help keep these pests in check.

In recent years, many people have become interested in keeping owls as pets. However, owls do not do well in captivity. Unlike parrots and many other pet birds, they do not talk or sing and are not very friendly. They also need to be fed whole, live animals on a regular basis.

*Owls often live near humans, sometimes even in the same buildings where people live.*

# What Does the Future Hold?

While most owls are thriving in their natural habitats, several species are endangered. They do not face many threats in the wild. Instead, human activity is the reason for the decrease in their population. One of the biggest problems that owls face is habitat loss. As human populations grow, people cut down more and more forests. They do this to clear space for homes, businesses, and farms. They also use the trees to make wood and paper products. With nowhere to live, some forest owl species are dying out.

Poison is another threat to some owl species. People often spray yards and fields with poisons that are meant to kill insects, rodents, and other pests. Unfortunately, these poisons can also hurt owls.

One way you can help owls is to build nest boxes in your yard. These boxes give owls a place to lay their eggs and raise their young. With a little help, all owls will have plenty of room to fly and hunt.

*Different owls need nest boxes of various sizes. Young tawny owls such as this one need larger boxes.*

# Words to Know

camouflage (KAM-o-flaj) — coloring or body shape that allows an animal to blend in with its surroundings

captivity (kap-TIV-i-tee) — the condition of being held or trapped by people

carnivores (KAR-nih-vorz) — animals that have meat as a regular part of their diet

clutch (KLUHCH) — a nest of eggs

courtship (KORT-ship) — the process of attracting and bonding with a mate

digest (dye-JEST) — to break down food in the organs of digestion so that it can be absorbed into the blood and used by the body

endangered (en-DAYN-jurd) — at risk of becoming extinct, usually because of human activity

extinct (ik-STINGKT) — no longer found alive

families (FAM-uh-leez) — groups of living things that are related to each other

fossils (FOSS-uhlz) — the hardened remains of prehistoric plants and animals

habitats (HAB-uh-tats) — the places where an animal or a plant is usually found

mates (MAYTS) — animals that join with other animals to reproduce

monogamous (muh-NAH-guh-muhs) — the practice of staying with the same mate for life

nocturnal (nahk-TUR-nuhl) — active mainly at night

perching (PUR-ching) — sitting or standing on the edge of something, often high up

predators (PREH-duh-turz) — animals that live by hunting other animals for food

preen (PREEN) — to clean and arrange feathers with the bill

prey (PRAY) — an animal that's hunted by another animal for food

pupils (PYOO-puhlz) — the round, black centers of eyes that allow light in

regurgitates (ri-GUR-ji-tayts) — brings food from the stomach back up to the mouth

serrated (SEHR-a-ted) — having a jagged edge

solitary (SOL-ih-tehr-ee) — preferring to live alone

species (SPEE-sheez) — one of the groups into which animals and plants of the same genus are divided

talons (TAL-uhnz) — sharp claws of a bird

territorial (terr-uh-TOR-ee-uhl) — defensive of a certain area

vocal (VOH-kuhl) — of or having to do with the voice

# Habitat Map

NORTH AMERICA

PACIFIC

OCEAN

ATLANTIC

SOUTH AMERICA

Owl Range

ARCTIC OCEAN

ASIA

EUROPE

AFRICA

PACIFIC
OCEAN

INDIAN

OCEAN

OCEAN

AUSTRALIA

# Find Out More

Books

Gish, Melissa. *Owls*. Mankato, MN: Creative Education, 2012.

Read, Tracy C. *Exploring the World of Owls*. Richmond Hill, ON, Canada: Firefly Books, 2011.

Thomson, Ruth. *The Life Cycle of an Owl*. New York: Rosen Publishing Group/ PowerKids Press, 2009.

Winnick, Nick. *Owls*. New York: AV2, 2010.

Visit this Scholastic Web site for more information on owls:
**www.factsfornow.scholastic.com**
Enter the keyword **Owls**

# Index

Page numbers in *italics* indicate a photograph or map.

*(Index continued)*

# About the Author

Josh Gregory writes and edits books for kids. He lives in Chicago, Illinois.